# ELLIOTT

ISBN-13: 978-1-4234-4655-2
ISBN-10: 1-4234-4655-0

HAL•LEONARD® CORPORATION

7777 W. BLUEMOUND RD. P.O. BOX 13819 MILWAUKEE, WI 53213

For all works contained herein:
Unauthorized copying, arranging, adapting,
recording or public performance is an infringement of copyright.
Infringers are liable under the law.

Visit Hal Leonard Online at
www.halleonard.com

# MOVIN' ON

Words and Music by ELLIOTT YAMIN, LEOR DIMANT,
OLIVER GOLDSTEIN and E. WEISFELD

Copyright © 2007 Sony/ATV Tunes LLC, Sing Like Yamin It, Sony/ATV Songs LLC, Lethal Dose Music, Ollie G Music and EJ Music
All Rights on behalf of Sony/ATV Tunes LLC, Sing Like Yamin It, Sony/ATV Songs LLC and Lethal Dose Music
Administered by Sony/ATV Music Publishing, 8 Music Square West, Nashville, TN 37203
International Copyright Secured   All Rights Reserved

# WAIT FOR YOU

Words and Music by MIKKEL ERIKSEN,
TOR ERIK HERMANSEN and PHILL "TAJ" JACKSON

© 2007 EMI MUSIC PUBLISHING LTD., RICH WATER, SONY\ATV MUSIC PUBLISHING UK LTD. and STELLAR SONGS LTD.
All Rights for EMI MUSIC PUBLISHING LTD. and RICH WATER in the U.S. and Canada Controlled and Administered by EMI APRIL MUSIC INC.
All Rights for SONY/ATV MUSIC PUBLISHING UK LTD. Administered by SONY/ATV MUSIC PUBLISHING, 8 Music Square West, Nashville, TN 37203
All Rights Reserved   International Copyright Secured   Used by Permission

have to go? You could have let me know, so now I'm all a - lone. Girl,

you could have stayed but you would-n't give me a chance. With you not a - round _ it's a lit-tle bit more than

I can stand. Ooh. _____ And all my tears they keep run-ning down my face, why did you

turn a - way? So why does your pride _ make you run and hide? _ Are you
why can't we just _ start all o - ver a - gain, get it

12

# FIND A WAY

Words and Music by ELLIOTT YAMIN,
TONY REYES and E. WEISFELD

Copyright © 2007 Sony/ATV Tunes LLC, Sing Like Yamin It, Sony/ATV Songs LLC, Hitface Music and EJ Music
All Rights on behalf of Sony/ATV Tunes LLC, Sing Like Yamin It, Sony/ATV Songs LLC and Hitface Music
Administered by Sony/ATV Music Publishing, 8 Music Square West, Nashville, TN 37203
International Copyright Secured  All Rights Reserved

# ONE WORD

Words and Music by MIKKEL ERIKSEN, TOR ERIK HERMANSEN,
PHILLIP JACKSON, ESPEN LIND and AMUND BJORKLUND

Copyright © 2007 Sony/ATV Music Publishing UK Ltd., EMI Music Publishing Ltd., Rich Water and Stellar Songs Ltd.
All Rights on behalf of Sony/ATV Music Publishing, 8 Music Square West, Nashville, TN 37203
All Rights on behalf of EMI Music Publishing Ltd. and Rich Water in the U.S. and Canada Controlled and Administered by EMI April Music Inc.
All Rights on behalf of Stellar Songs Ltd. in the U.S. and Canada Controlled and Administered by EMI Blackwood Music Inc.
International Copyright Secured  All Rights Reserved

# YOU ARE THE ONE

Words and Music by ELLIOTT YAMIN, LEOR DIMANT, TONY REYES, JOHN O'BRIEN and OLIVER GOLDSTEIN

Some-times I sit and I won-
Be - fore you, I was so blind _

- der _ and I just can't seem _ to _ be - lieve _
I did - n't know which _ path _ to _ choose. _

Copyright © 2007 Sony/ATV Tunes LLC, Sing Like Yamin It, Sony/ATV Songs LLC, Lethal Dose Music,
Hitface Music, WB Music Corp., Tearskneekatmusic and Ollie G Music
All Rights on behalf of Sony/ATV Tunes LLC, Sing Like Yamin It, Sony/ATV Songs LLC, Lethal Dose Music and Hitface Music
Administered by Sony/ATV Music Publishing, 8 Music Square West, Nashville, TN 37203
International Copyright Secured   All Rights Reserved

# I'M THE MAN

Words and Music by MARSHALL ALTMAN
and PAUL FOX

**Slow Rock Ballad**

When I ___
When I ___

___ woke up with the ___ sun - light ___ and dreams ech - o - ing through ___ my head ___ and I ___
___ lay down and the ___ moon is bright at the end of a work - ing day, ___ got a ___

___ heard you breath - ing ___ soft - ly, ___ I re - mem - bered the things ___ you said. ___ There is ___
___ feel - ing, I be - lieve it, ___ and I won't let it slip ___ a - way. ___ There is ___

*\* Recorded a half step higher.*

© 2007 EMI APRIL MUSIC INC., GALT LINE MUSIC and PAUL FOX MUSIC
All Rights for GALT LINE MUSIC Controlled and Administered by EMI APRIL MUSIC INC.
All Rights Reserved   International Copyright Secured   Used by Permission

I'm the man who won't let you down. 'Cause I'm the man in love with

**Repeat and Fade**

you.
*(Vocal 1st time only)*

**Optional Ending**

you.

# TRAIN WRECK

Words and Music by ELLIOTT YAMIN,
DEREK BRAMBLE and MICHELLE LEWIS

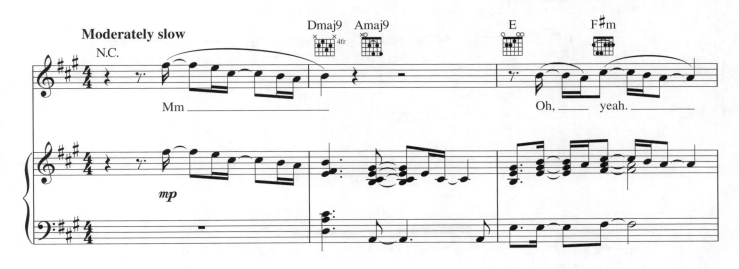

Mm _____

Oh, ____ yeah. _____

We're head-in' for a train wreck. ___

I got-ta be hon-est with you, ba - by, I knew it right from the start. ___

Copyright © 2007 Sony/ATV Tunes LLC, Sing Like Yamin It, Dimensional Music Of 1091, Kodikaysi Music and Bea The Dog Music
All Rights on behalf of Sony/ATV Tunes LLC and Sing Like Yamin It Administered by Sony/ATV Music Publishing, 8 Music Square West, Nashville, TN 37203
Worldwide Rights on behalf of Dimensional Music Of 1091 and Kodikaysi Music Administered by Cherry Lane Music Publishing Company, Inc.
International Copyright Secured   All Rights Reserved

# FREE

Words and Music by KEVIN RISTO, WAYNNE NUGENT,
LOUIS BIANCANIELLO, SAMUEL WATTERS,
ROBERT DANIELS and MARLAINA KEMP

Copyright © 2007 Sony/ATV Tunes LLC, Break North Music, Waynne Writers, S.M.Y. Publishing, EMI April Music Inc.,
Breakthrough Creations, EMI Virgin Songs, Inc., Bigg Kidd Music and Mar'Laina Yashene Kemp Publishing
All Rights on behalf of Sony/ATV Tunes LLC, Break North Music, Waynne Writers and S.M.Y. Publishing
Administered by Sony/ATV Music Publishing, 8 Music Square West, Nashville, TN 37203
All Rights on behalf of Breakthrough Creations Controlled and Administered by EMI April Music Inc.
All Rights on behalf of Bigg Kidd Music Controlled and Administered by EMI Virgin Songs, Inc.
International Copyright Secured   All Rights Reserved

# ALRIGHT

Words and Music by ELLIOTT YAMIN, LEOR DIMANT,
TONY REYES and OLIVER GOLDSTEIN

**Moderate Disco tempo**

If you want some-thing new, may-be I got what you need. _____
I see you from a-cross the room, hot e-nough to stop the beat. _____

And if you just wan-na groove, you can come get next to me. _____
And peo-ple com-in' up to you, but no-bod-y that you care to meet. _____

Well ba-by, I'm tried and true; what you get is what you see. _____
Some-thing a-bout the way you move is turn-ing up the heat. _____

Copyright © 2007 Sony/ATV Tunes LLC, Sing Like Yamin It, Sony/ATV Songs LLC, Lethal Dose Music, Hitface Music and Ollie G Music
All Rights on behalf of Sony/ATV Tunes LLC, Sing Like Yamin It, Sony/ATV Songs LLC, Lethal Dose Music and Hitface Music
Administered by Sony/ATV Music Publishing, 8 Music Square West, Nashville, TN 37203
International Copyright Secured   All Rights Reserved

may-be for a min-ute we can in-dis-creet-ly slip out of sight, _____ aw ba-

-by. You're so right, _____ aw \_\_\_\_ ba - by. I

can't get you out of that place in my mind \_\_\_\_ that makes a man cra-zy e-nough to

make him want to do it all night, _____ ba - by. You're so fine. \_\_

# TAKE MY BREATH AWAY

Words and Music by DAVID RYAN HARRIS
and AL ANDERSON

Copyright © 2006 Songs Of Windswept Pacific, Peace Pourage Music and Mommy A Monster Music
All Rights Administered by Songs Of Windswept Pacific
All Rights Reserved   Used by Permission

need to take some time _____ and see _____ where this is go - ing.

Girl, it feels so right _____ when we hold __ each oth - er tight. _____

Tell me it's

# A SONG FOR YOU

Words and Music by
LEON RUSSELL

**Slowly, with feeling**

I've been _ so man-y plac - es _ in my

life and time. _    I've sung _ a lot of songs    and I've made some bad _ rhymes. _

I've act - ed out my life _ on stag - es    with ten thou-sand peo - ple watch - ing.

Copyright © 1970 IRVING MUSIC, INC.
Copyright Renewed
All Rights Reserved    Used by Permission